Farquhar Maclennan

Fearchair-a-Ghunna

The Ross-Shire Wanderer - His Life And Saying

Farquhar Maclennan

Fearchair-a-Ghunna
The Ross-Shire Wanderer - His Life And Saying

ISBN/EAN: 9783744691925

Printed in Europe, USA, Canada, Australia, Japan

Cover: Foto ©ninafisch / pixelio.de

More available books at **www.hansebooks.com**

Fearchair-a-Ghunna

THE

ROSS-SHIRE WANDERER,

HIS

LIFE AND SAYINGS,

BY

The Author of "The Maid of Fairburn," etc., etc.

SECOND EDITION—ENLARGED.

INVERNESS:
JOHN NOBLE, CASTLE STREET.
1887.

CONTENTS.

Chapter.	Page.
I. Early Life	1
II. The Wanderer	9
III. Eccentricities	19
IV. Self Esteem	30
V. Ingenuity	39
VI. Quaint Remarks	46
VII. Gravity and Death	59

FEARCHAIR-A-GHUNNA

THE ROSS-SHIRE WANDERER.

CHAPTER I.—EARLY LIFE.

Birth-Place—Education—Personal Appearance—Incipient Eccentricity—Story of Early Life—Smuggling—Burning the Gauger's Cottage—His Brother's Death—Punishing the Informer—Adrift.

Farquhar Maclennan, *alias* Fearchair-a-Ghunna was born in Strathconon, Ross-shire, in the year 1784, and spent his youth in that district. Little is known regarding his life during that period, and probably it was as uneventful as were the lives of his neighbours in the beautiful strath mentioned. His father, a well-to-do crofter, as crofters went, did not think it necessary to burden his children with a school education, and even had the idea occurred to him there were few facilities for carrying it out. Poor Farquhar was therefore so destitute of literary attainments that, to the day of his death he could not distinguish A from B. His knowledge of the English language was also very limited, the only words he assayed being "yes," and "no." But though thus unlearned and unaccomplished, young Farquhar received the elements of a more practical education on the farm and on the moor. Shooting, smuggliing, and agriculture appear to have been the three principal pursuits of the district in those times, and in the two first of these the subject of this sketch took great delight.

Farquhar's personal appearance was quite in keeping with his character and mode of life. He was somewhat low in stature, but firmly built, with broad square shoulders, and, at this period, a gait remarkably erect and almost stately. His head was covered with a profusion of long bristly hair, which seldom or never saw a comb. His eyes were small, restless, and piercing, while a fixed determination was stamped on his care-worn countenance.

It is not now known whether in his early youth Farquhar was subject to that aberration of intellect which in latter years caused him to take to a wandering life. The probability is that it was of gradual growth, though its progress was eventually hastened by the troubles resulting from the smuggling propensities of the family. There is one story told of Farquhar's youth which indicates that he had begun even this early to show symptoms of mental disease or eccentricty.

It was in the spring season of the year, and Farquhar's father, who had no grain-seed for his croft, sent him for a supply of seed to Strathpeffer, which was famed for the purity of its barley. A journey from Strathconon to Strathpeffer at the time in question was no easy task, for the road between those places was very different from the one there now. However, Farquhar at length reached his destination, got the barley, put it on his back and returned home. He arrived at Strathconon about midnight, and, finding that his father had retired to bed, he set to work and sowed the barley. Although the people of Strathconon were not early risers, their fowls were, and every hen chicken, and cock, within reach of Farquhar's newly-sown barley were picking it up for hours ere a single person in the Strath had got up. It was towards evening when Farquhar told that he had sown the barley, and by that time almost every grain of it had been picked off the ground. When his father chided him for having sown the barley during the night, he readily replied:—

"He who would have a good crop, and an early harvest, must be up betimes. Had you risen in time in the morning, and harrowed the ground the fowls could not have eaten the seed." For this answer his father gave him such a severe castigation that it is supposed to have injuriously affected his naturally feeble mind.

Another and a different story told of one of the causes that led to the weakness of intellect he displayed, belongs to this period. We gave it as related by a Redcastle neighbour of our hero's When a lad, Fearchair was engaged as a herd by a Ferintosh Farmer. His master was a man very exacting in his demands for early rising on the part of his servants; he could not get enough of work out of them. At the earliest break of day he was rousing them up. Fearchair and the ploughman resolved to play a trick on their employer, and one night in the harvest time they cut a lot of divots and built up his bedroom window so as to totally exclude the chance of daylight penetrating. The farmer got up several times during the early morning, and as often retired to bed, as the daylight had not appeared. At last he began to suspect a trick had been played on him, and dressing himself went to the door, when the mid-day sunshine burst on him. He then examined the window and discovering the cause of the darkness, he was greatly enraged. He rushed into the farm yard and seized a spade; the first one he met was Fearchair, and lifting the weapon he struck him on the top of the head with the the flat side. It is said that from that time Farquhar's weakness of understanding became more marked.

Fearchair seems to have been remarkable unfortunate in his engagements when a youth. After leaving the service of this Ferrintosh farmer, he engaged as a herd with a man named Gray, at Croftruny, in the parish of Redcastle. While tending his charge one warm day in summer, he lay down on the soft grass, and, as herds frequently do, he fell asleep. The consequence was that his cattle, one after another, went into a cornfield close by. Gray noticed the cattle in the corn, and, after driving them out of it, found poor Fearchair in the land of dreams, and without making any attempt to awaken him, struck him a blow on the side of the head with a spade he was carrying at the time. The blow broke the sleeper's collar-bone and made an ugly gash in the upper part of his cheek, the scar of which he carried while he lived.

About eighty years ago, smuggling was carried on extensively in all parts of the Highlands and Islands of Scotland, but in no part, it is said, did it attain such a height as in Strathconon, where it entirely superseded every lawful branch of industry. It proved a curse rather than a blessing to the quiet inhabitants of the Strath, profiting none but ruining many. The Strathconon smugglers, like their neighbours, the smugglers of Strathcarron, transacted most of their business with the citizens of Inverness, whither they always went during the night; and many a bloody encounter took place between themselves and the Excise Officers, the latter generally coming off second best. Ultimately the fame of Strathconon as a place of illicit distillation had spread far and wide, and the Board of Excise resolved to station a staff of Officers in the district in order, if possible, to put a stop to the illegal trade. A cottage near the scene of operations was procured and put into order for the reception of the exciseman and his staff, but when the repairs were all but completed, the cottage, which was thatched with heather, was found one morning a heap of ashes having been burnt during the night. That this was the work of an incendiary there was no doubt whatever; and every person in the Strath knew that Farquhar had something to do with it, though no one could be induced to divulge the fact. The Excise Officers were most zealous in their efforts to discover the guilty party but they were completely foiled in their endeavours. Farquhar being known as a leading smuggler was apprehended on suspicion and brought to Dingwall, but, although he was subjected to a most searching examination on the way thither, nothing was elicited from him. At Dingwall various schemes of examining him were adopted with the view of extorting anything he might know regarding the burning of the cottage, but to no purpose; he was as mute as a lamb, and gazed at his inquisitors unconcernedly. They were consequently forced to release him. The Excise Officers were armed with cutlasses in those days, and, in order to extort a confession from Farquhar, the Exciseman of the district declared that he would cut off his head unless he gave the desired information. "You may get all the information from my head that you can," said Farquhar, "but you will get none from me." Notwithstanding the vigilance of the excise officers placed in the glen, smuggling was still carried on in Strathconon, and one of the most notorious defenders was a brother of Farquhar Maclennan's. This individual was one of the strongest men in the Strath—and there were some herculeans in Strathconon in those days—but in an encounter with the gaugers he was accidentally killed. This circumstance excited Farquhar to an extraordinary degree, and he vowed he would be revenged for the death of his brother, whom he loved intensely. It is said that he watched by day and night for an opportunity to kill the man whom he regarded as his brother's murderer, but he does not seem to have got that opportunity. From that time, however, Farquhar Maclennan was a changed man.

But the smuggling troubles of the Maclennan family were not yet over. A treacherous neighbour betrayed to the excise officers the site of their illicit distillery, and one dark night old Maclennan was caught red-handed at the illegal work. He was taken to Dingwall and heavily fined, while the implements and produce found on the spot were confiscated. In his rage at this untoward event, Farquhar was easily prevailed on by his comrades to revenge himself on the informer by setting fire to his house and steading.

It is said that Farquhar's imbecility was at this time feigned to screen him from the consequence of his offence, but we have seen that on a former occasion he showed signs of derangement. The truth seems to be that these accumulating troubles all combined to cloud his spirit. He now began to think that he was marked out for some dread judgement, and ultimately he gave way to his terrors. Without informing any one of his intention, he wandered out into the world to search for the peace of mind which he could not obtain on the banks of the Conon. Farquhar was twenty-five years of age, when, one fine day towards the end of the spring of 1809, he turned his back on the home of his childhood. He never returned to it again or expressed a longing to see it, until he neared the end of his earthly pilgrimage, and then he merely asked that his body should be laid with the dust of his forefathers in the old Church-yard at Strathconon. Yet he never forgot his home and kindred, nor showed any shame for the records of his family. When asked from whom he was descended, he always replied readily and proudly—" I am sprung from the Smugglers of Strathconon."

CHAPTER II.—THE WANDERER.

A Vagabond Life—Farquhar's Dress—Accoutrements—Gun—Gatherings—Mode of Travelling—Kessock Ferry—The Railway—Culloden—Fairburn—Kilcoy.

A Wandering life in the Highlands during the first half of this century was a very different thing from modern trampism. The Highland rover in old times was generally a more or less interesting object, and in the absence of poor laws, he could generally count on a hospitable reception. Some of the wanderers—and Farquhar was one of these—declined to be classed with common beggars, but on the contrary set up as gentlemen-at-large to entertain whom should be considered not a trouble but an honour.

When Farquhar had bidden farewell to Strathconon, he travelled for some time through various parts of Ross-shire where he neither worked nor lacked, but ultimately he began to confine his tours to the Black Isle and the opposite shores of the Beauly Firth. Throughout that district he soon became a general favourite especially among the young folk, and never was in want of food, or of tobacco, the only luxury for which he showed a fondness.

Farquhar's dress was so fantastic that a description of it must be given. He wore a blue Kilmarnock bonnet, replaced in his later years by a wide-awake hat, but it would often be difficult to say what was the shape or character of his head-gear, so completely hidden would it be under the profusion of feathers, bits of paper, and other ornaments which he stuck thereon. A substantial iron chain fastened under the chin kept the head-dress in position. His clothes were generally of various bright colours and secured by another heavy chain, or iron-wire girdle passing round his body. In his wanderings he picked up all the pieces of old metal, bones, rags, paper, and feathers he came across, and these he pinned and tied on his clothing and carried about with him for days and weeks together. When thoroughly covered with these decorations he resembled a large bundle of rags and filthy matter, rather than a human being.

But the other parts of his outfit were no less extraordinary. The burden of flotsam and jetsam which he generally carried was firmly bound on his shoulders with numberless chains. A brace of cast-away pistols hung at his iron belt, also a Mexican powder-horn, several iron hoops, pieces of chain, and a bunch of keys. During one part of his career an old sword was added to his other accoutrements but it disappeared, probably because it was too good for daily wear.

But the great characteristic feature of

Farquhar's appearance was his gun. He had an over-weening fondness for guns, and was never without one—hence the appellation of Fearchair-a-Ghunna, "Farquhar of the Gun," by which he was generally known. Usually Farquhar's gun was of the most wonderful construction. During the earlier period of his wandering life he carried half-a-dozen old gun barrels, tied together with a string or chain, in such a way that they resembled a rude monster revolver, the stock of which was formed by himself, of the thick end of a tree, and was about as heavy as a man could lift off the ground. Even Farquhar found it too heavy to use at the shoulder, and so he got a rest made for it. He also carried a pan with a burning peat to fire the powder. The operation in firing was first to get the gun adjusted on the rest to the requisite level, then to lay a train of powder to each of the six barrels, and lastly to apply the peat. The six barrels went off simultaneously, causing a tremendous report but seldom if ever doing anything more serious. From the following incident it may be surmised that, Fearchair himself in his secret soul felt that his weapon was not so useful as a simpler gun might be. One day he met the Redcastle gamekeeper, who was carrying a beautiful single-barrel gun on his shoulder. Fearchair expressed a desire to see his gun, and was at once gratified. After examining it carefully, he proposed that they might with advantage make an exchange. "My gun," he said, " would be of immense service to you." You should have six guns instead of one, and what havock that would do among the moor fowls." We need hardly say that the keeper declined to strike a bargain with him. The gun which Fearchair carried in his later years was also of the most unique description— an old rusty barrel without either lock or stock, but there were some changes in his mode of handling it. As soon as he saw a crow near the road side, he would take aim, and holding the gun thus, his next proceeding was to light a match and apply it to the touch-hole.

Fearchair was a great gatherer; nothing came amiss for his burden, and all sorts of articles that were thrown away as worthless were collected by him and stored in his house. For some of these articles he found a ready market in Inverness, and accordingly he paid periodic visits to that town to sell his wares. A great part of them however consisted of the merest rubbish, and these things were hoarded up with miserly care. This was particularly the case with pretty stones which he picked up on his travels, and of which several cart loads were found in his house after his demise. It should be added that his burden very generally contained a dead fowl or rabbit found by the wayside.

Farquhar's load would often be more than sufficient for a donkey, but he always trudged along on foot, seldom trusting himself to any other mode of locomotion. Though cumbered with his goods to such an extent that it really seemed a wonder how he could move at all, the wanderer travelled, and even danced, with an agility that was truly amazing. On reaching Beauly on his way to Inverness with a burden of goods, one fine summer day, he was met by some of the crew of a vessel which was about to leave for Inverness. The day been warm and his load heavy, they prevailed on him to take a passage in the vessel. Shortly after he had stepped on board, and when the vessel was just loosing from the wharf, he overheard some of the crew saying, that they were bound for Newcastle. This was only a ruse to frighten him, but he had scarcely heard it when he was standing on the quay, having cleared the ship's bulwarks and the open space betwixt the vessel and the quay with a bound, burden and all. As soon as he got on *terra firma*, Fearchair in unmeasured terms denounced the sailors for attempting to carry him away, and even declared that, if he had it in his power, he would send them to the bottom.

The Ross-shire Wanderer was so attached to his burden, that though it were never so heavy it was utterly impossible to induce him to lay it off his back—even when resting, or when crossing Kessock Ferry, as the following anecdote will show. He was passing east High Street, Inverness, one day, with a heavy burden of his customary ware, and when opposite a woollen and yarn warehouse, immediately to the east of the Market Brae, he was accosted by an acquaintance, who asked him if he had come across Kessock Ferry. "No," said the Wanderer, "I have not. These Ferrymen are so peculiar that they don't care to see me going into their boat with my bundle, and, besides, I am so tormented at the Ferry, by passengers and others, that I am disgusted to go that way. I came round by Beauly—but oh! man, what a lot of yarn is there (pointing to the warehouse.) It would be grand for wafts and warps!"

Fearchair was an old man before the railway was introduced into the district and he never travelled by it. He was once however on the point of doing so, but the result of the attempt was not of a kind to induce him to try it again. It was some time after the opening of the Ross-shire line and Fearchair was in Inverness selling his goods. A certain wag with whom he was acquainted, met him on the street, and advised him to go to the station and take the train for Tarradale. Fearchair for some time refused to do so, but at length consented. He went to the station, and took his seat in one of the carriages of the north-going train, but he was hardly seated when the ticket collector came round and demanded his ticket. Poor Fearchair had nothing of the kind, for his adviser had meanly omitted to supply him with one, and so he was ruthlessly dragged out of the carriage, and left sprawling on the platform. As soon as he recovered his equilibrium, he grinned and said—" This road reminds me of the Lord's Table—no one is permitted to take it, unless he is provided with a token or ticket."

During a long period of his wanderings in the Black Isle, Fearchair was accommodated, when so disposed, in an out-house belonging to the Manse at Redcastle. But one day he took it into his head that some of the domestics of the manse had, during his absence, tampered with his goods; and determining to be revenged, he retaliated by stealing the plough irons and destroying the minister's potatoes. He accomplished the latter in this manner. He made holes with his staff in the roofs of the potato pits, and then carried salt-water from the sea and poured it into the holes thus made until the potato pits were flooded. It need scarcely be said that the potatoes were completely destroyed. For this offence Fearchair was apprehended and brought before the Sheriff at Dingwall, but he was immediately discharged, as the proof against him was insufficient. It is related that when the Sheriff asked him why he did it. Fearchair answered—" Well, Sheriff, would you not punish the man that would destroy your books and papers?" On returning to Killearnan he told the Minister, the Rev. Mr Macrae, that he had lived at Redcastle before him, and that he would probably do so after him, adding—"I would advise you Mr Macrae to take good care of yourself." Mr Macrae had a favourite Newfoundland dog, and shortly afterwards it was found dead. On its being dissected, its lungs were found pierced with upwards of a hundred pins. It would appear that Fearchair had administered a doze to the dog, consisting of leaven filled with pins. The minister could stand this conduct no longer, and one day while Fearchair was absent, he set several men and horses to work, and the whole contents of Fearchair's domicile were carted into the sea. When Fearchair returned, and found that his precious goods were gone, his rage knew no bounds, and he left the place declaring that he would be revenged on the minister. This threat he carried out by stealing everything left insecured about the premises, and tossing them into the sea. It may be observed that Fearchair's remark, that he would probably be in Redcastle after the minister, was substantiated for he was sometimes there, many years after the clergyman had left it. Fearchair lived many years in an old house at Tarradale, but latterly he occupied a house built for him by Mr Maclennan, Hilton, and here he amassed a store of stones, metal, bones, rags, and old shoes that completely filled up the interior, until there was scarcely enough space left for him to turn about in.

He ascertained while serving a Ferrintosh farmer, that, that property belonged to Mr Forbes of Culloden ; and in acknowledgement of the kind treatment he received on that estate, he went periodically to Culloden House, to pay, as he used to say, his respects to the " good proprietor." Fearchair's visits to Culloden were always longed for and appreciated by the servants, to whom his uncouth appearance, with his load of rags and iron, afforded great amusement. And not less so did his curt answers to all their queries, as he sat on a form beside the massive table in the kitchen, his keen eyes watching their every movement.

Fearchair frequently visited Fairburn House also, and he was never allowed to go away without first receiving a good meal. It happened on one occasion that the cook coaxed him to take more food than was good for him, and the result was, that he soon became uncomfortable, and at length ran out to the lawn, where he began to roll himself on the grass in great agony, exclaiming vociferously—" Lord God Almighty, put an end at once to my miserable life, for I am in dreadful pain." He then began to abuse the cook in good round terms for having given him so much of her good things, and declared that he would be avenged for what she had done.

The Wanderer frequently visited the house of a farmer in the heights of Kilcoy, who successfully carried on the same trade which Fearchair followed in his earlier years, namely, smuggling. On the occasion of these visits, he always received as much of John Barley-Corn as he liked to take, and, invariably finished off by a dance. As he never laid down his burden, this performance afforded the greatest possible sport to the scores of young people who assembled there, for the express purpose of seeing him dance. He would continue the exercise for about an hour, his chains and hoops supplying the music.

Like many other weak-minded persons, poor Fearchair was sometimes imposed upon by unprincipled persons. After a round through the Aird, and a call at Beaufort Castle, he came one evening to Beauly with a heavy load of goods on his back, and his purse pretty well replenished. On reaching the village he called at a shop and made some little purchases, and then left for Tarradale. He had not been long away from the shop, when he returned, and told the merchant that he was accosted by two men near the Muir of Ord Market Stance, who robbed him of his purse and its contents. Having described the robbers, the merchant had no difficulty in recognising them as two drunken characters who were in his shop when Fearchair made his purchases, and had evidently observed where he put his purse. Otherwise they would have had no small difficulty in finding its *locus*, for Fearchair was always so well padded with his heterogeneous burden that it would take all the skill of a Scotland-yard detective to find a particular article. The thieves were strangers in the district, and the merchant did not think it worth while to set the police on their track—he thought they would be sufficiently punished if one half of Fearchair's anathema's fell upon them—for the Wanderer earnestly implored heaven not to let them pass unpunished.

CHAPTER III.— ECCENTRICITIES.

"The Garrison"—Food—The Major's Dog—Gunpowder—Shooting Incident—The Strike Fire—Shooting Accidents—Hunting a Donkey—Stone Blasting—"Guard your Life."—In Beauly Ferry—"Smoking" the Rooks.

Fearchair-a-Ghunna was full of whims and oddities, and though generally able to take care of himself, he seemed incapable of doing anything like other people. We have already seen how eccentric he was in regard to clothing and personal habits, and his views on dwellings were no less extraordinary. After being ejected from the minister's out-house at Redcastle, Fearchair went to the Muir of Tarradale, where he found an old deserted hut of which he took possession. It was of the most primitive construction; the walls formed of boulders and sods, were low and thick; the roof was thatched with broom, brackens, and heather, and the interior consisted of one apartment. This tenement Fearchair proceeded to furnish in accordance with his own notions on such subjects, but the greater part of it was occupied by his accumulating rubbish. He named it the "Garrison," and was at great pains to protect it against burglars. He was somewhat indisposed at one time, and, thinking that he was about to die, he set to and built up the door of this house with stones, so as to make it a tomb. He afterwards said that he wished his body to be left in the "Garrison" till the day of judgment, but he expressed a different wish before he died.

In regard to food Fearchair was anything but fastidious. He often ate the bodies of fowls and rabbits raw, and sometimes, though a house were quite near at hand, he preferred to light a fire in the open air, and roast parts of grouse and rooks that had died by accident, and that he had picked up by the way, which he devoured greedily. He even liked to eat frogs; but he did not like to see them looking so steadfastly at him while he was devouring them. He, therefore, made it a point to take out their eyes first and then eat them! It need hardly be said that, this food was anything but wholesome, more especially as it was neither cleaned nor properly dressed. He called a ditch that passed through a certain marshy place in the parish of Redcastle, "the red herring fishing grounds," on account of the large number of frogs that existed in it.

It is said that Fearchair's unscrupulous voracity sometimes made him acquainted with strange companions, and the following story is in point. There lived in Ross-shire a certain Major for whom Fearchair entertained no great favour. It happened on one occasion, that an old horse lay dead in the neighbourhood of the Major's residence, and Fearchair went for a piece of the carcase. On reaching it, he found the Major's dog helping himself to a good repast. Fearchair at once began to help himself too, but immediately he commenced the dog began to growl. "Ah!" said Fearchair, "'*sann ort tha drein a Mhadsair*," *i. e.* "the Major's snarl is on your face. Keep to your own side man," Fearchair continued, addressing the dog. "I will put a line between us (drawing a line on the carcase), I won't pass it, and I hope you won't come over it either."

Fearchair had a particular fondness for gunpowder, in fact there was nothing else that he loved so well. He often said that next to his Creator there was no object that he venerated so much, and he would range all the gamekeepers houses for miles around for a supply of the coveted article. The taste was very likely formed in his old poaching days in Strathconon, but it continued strong, even when the frailities of age rendered its gratification difficult. We have already seen how largely his shooting appliances bulked on his attention, and he took an extraordinary pleasure in using them. But with weapons so cumbrous, it is not surprising that Fearchair could kill nothing. His own opinion was however, that he was a first-class shot, and if he fired at anything it must certainly be killed. One incident out of a hundred will illustrate this. He was rambling one day in the neighbourhood of Brahan Castle, and happening to see a crow close to him he fired at it. On hearing the report of the gun, the crow, of course, flew away as merry and hale as ever. About a month afterwards, Fearchair was strolling near Redcastle—miles away, and finding a dead crow which had been shot by some of the gamekeepers, he picked it up exclaiming:—

"Look here, look here! this is the very crow that I shot at Brahan Castle. I aimed well, and I knew I had killed it, though I could not find it." He cooked the crow in the open air and ate it!

As has been already remarked, Fearchair carried about with him a vessel containing a burning peat for the purpose of firing his gun, for lucifer matches were unknown during the earlier part of his wandering life, and his gun was not suited for any other means of igniting the powder. But one day he went to a blacksmith's shop and told vulcan that, he, sometimes, lost good chances of shooting crows on account of the fire in his peat being extinguished by rain, or from other causes, and asked him whether he could invent something that would answer his purpose instead of the peat. The blacksmith answered that he could easily invent an instrument, and that he would make it, and give it to him ere he left the shop, if he would first say his peculiar prayer—*Urnuigh na Creubhaiy.* Fearchair readily agreed, and repeated this remarkable prayer, which will be found in Chapter VII. of this sketch. When Fearchair had finished his prayer, the blacksmith began, and soon formed a piece of steel to suit Fearchair's wrist, on which it was securely tied with a strong leathern thong. Vulcan then instructed him how to strike a piece of flint against the steel when he wanted a light. This piece of steel was never removed from Fearchair's wrist, either by day or by night, until he became ill.

Some of Fearchair's sporting experiences were not of a very pleasant kind. On one occasion he met with a rather severe accident, when at a wild duck hunt. Having charged his six barreled gun, he proceeded to a part of the beach near Redcastle, which he knew to be frequented by a number of wild-ducks. After lying on the shore for some time a few ducks came within range. He fired, and the next instant he was lying senseless on the shore. One or two of the barrels, being overcharged, had burst, and some of the pieces striking Fearchair on the head and face, cut him dreadfully. How long he lay insensible on the shore he did not know, but, although he lost a large quantity of blood, he soon recovered. Fearchair's gun seems to have had a penchant for bursting On another occasion he was passing a field where a man was ploughing with a pair of horses. Fearchair noticed a crow and fired at it; but, from some unaccountable cause, the gun burst, and flew in pieces through the air. One piece of the barrel struck the ground close to the ploughman's feet, and a bystander asked Fearchair how his gun had burst, pointing out that he had nearly killed a man. "Oh"! said Fearchair, "the man was wise enough to keep out of the way. He knew that these old muskets could not be trusted. I never made one, and if they chance to break, I am not to blame."

On one of his rounds he called one day at the Mill of S—, and the miller there, a jocular sort of fellow, addressing him said :—" I don't see what is the use of you going about with that lockless musket, Fearchair. I will allow you to kill my dog, man, if you can." *An cum thu dhomh e. v.* or "will you hold him (the dog) for me?" asked Fearchair eagerly. "I will, indeed," answered the miller, as he seized the dog and held it for Fearchair to fire at it. Fearchair at once levelled his musket at the animal, and began to blow the fire in the peat, which he kept close to the priming. The explosion at length took place, and several pieces of the pot-metal, with which the musket was charged, penetrated the ground at the miller's feet, frightening him almost out of his wits. One metal splinter struck the dog's back, tearing off a piece of the skin and flesh. The poor animal, as might be expected, ran frantically away, howling madly with pain and fear, to the no small amusement of the subject of our sketch. The miller candidly acknowledged that he had acted very foolishly, and declared that had he known that the musket contained any other thing than powder, he would not for the world have done what he then did.

As Fearchair was passing along a road at the base of a hill on one occasion, he, noticed some quadruped browsing a little distance up the hill. He at once charged his gun, and cautiously approached the animal until he got within a reasonable distance of it, when he applied the match in his usual way, and bang went the shot. The quadruped was, of course, not touched, but on hearing the loud report of the gun, it was frightened and ran away. Thinking that he had wounded the animal, Fearchair gave chase for the purpose of bagging his game. But the harder Fearchair ran, the swifter ran the animal. Fearchair continued thus, chasing the animal the whole day. At length, weary and fatigued the latter made for a house in the valley, and by the time it reached, Fearchair was close at its heels. " Hollo," cried the occupier of the house, on seeing Fearchair running after the beast. " Why are you running after my ass, Fearchair?" " It's a stag that I shot on the hill," said the hunter of the ass, " and I have been running after him the whole day." It was some time before the man could convince

Fearchair that he was really chasing an ass, instead of a stag. "The Ross-shire Wanderer" had never seen an ass before.

Fearchair-a-Ghunna had another way of using his beloved powder, and one which yielded him scarcely inferior pleasure. He spent much of his time in blasting stones for the Black Isle farmers, not for fee or reward, but merely on account of the childish delight he took in seeing and hearing the explosion when the powder was fired. It was most amusing to see this eccentric blaster at work. As soon as the match was applied to the fuse, he gave in stentorian tones the usual word of alarm "Fire." This he repeated several times, all the while running round the stone as hard as he could, and gradually enlarging the circle, until the explosion took place.

Fearchair's simplicity as well as his characteristic love for powder, are well illustrated by the following well authenticated anecdote. He was one day at the Muir of Ord market, where he saw two Ross-shire proprietors with whom he was well acquainted. Later in the day he noticed that they were joined by another gentleman whom he did not know. Fearchair dogged them for some little time, and when they separated for a moment, he steped up to one of the gentlemen with whom he was acquainted, and told him that he required some powder, and wished to ask their friend for some, but as the latter had no Gaelic, he was at a loss how to ask for it. "Go right up to him," said the Ross-shire proprietor, "present your gun to him, and say—"guard your life," and he will give you as much powder as you like." Fearchair at once went up to the stranger, who was an English gentleman, presented his gun, and in his usual gruff manner said :—"guard your life." The gentleman took such a fright that, he at once left the market, for although both the Ross shire gentlemen assured him that, Fearchair had no bad intention, and that it was they themselves that had put the words in his mouth, he would not be persuaded to stay.

Fearchair was one day returning home from Inverness and wishing to shorten his journey he went to Beauly ferry and asked two youths whom he found at the boat to ferry him across. They told him they would do so if he would first repeat *Urnuigh-na-Creubhaig*, but he was so disgusted, as already mentioned, by people asking him to say this prayer, that he refused them point blank. The youths being as obstinate as Fearchair himself, they kept him standing at the water's edge for a considerable time. At length, however, a party who was in a great hurry, came to the ferry, and at once leaped into the boat. But although he was heavily laden with his wares, Fearchair jumped into the boat as nimbly as any of the others and was at once rowed across. But the other passengers sprang out of the boat immediately on her bow touching the beach, and were hastening towards the village long ere Fearchair thought of leaving his seat. As soon as the other passengers left the boat the youths shoved out to the centre of the stream, notwithstanding Fearchair's remonstrances with them to the contrary. Finding that his appeals to be allowed ashore were disregarded, he sprang into the water and notwithstanding his heavy load of iron, his rags and big cloak floated him like a buoy. At length his feet touched the ground on the Inverness side of the ferry when he exclaimed, " Had I known that the ground was so near me I would have left your rotten craft long ago, you wicked vagabonds, *Mo mholachd oirbh*," that is my curse rest on you.

In the wood of Ardochy, parish of Urray, there was a rookery, and one day when Fearchair was in the height of his strength he took it into his head that, if he could smoke the rooks in much the same way as bees are smoked, he could have flesh sufficient to last him for twelve months. With this strange idea in his head, and having every thing prepared, he went to the rookery on one evening when it was dark, so that the rooks would not see him, and windy so that they would not hear, but when crossing the bridge of Orrin on his way to Ardochy, he was met by a boy from near Tarradale, whom Fearchair had nick-named "Nossing" (Nothing), on account of the manner in which he used to tease the Wanderer. " Is that you Fearchair ?" asked the boy when they met. " Yes, that is my name," answered Fearchair. "Are you Mr Nossing?" The boy replied in the affirmative, and they both sat down to rest at the end of the bridge. On "Nossing" learning where the other was going, he asked him for a penny worth of shot, at the same time showing Fearchair the penny. "Nossing" got a few grains of shot and offering Fearchair a bit stone in payment, ran off as fast as he could. "Nossing" had scarcely sat down in his father's house when Fearchair entered, swearing fearfully. "Is 'Nossing' in?" he enquired angrily of the boy's father. "Why are you asking for him?" demanded the other. "To shot him as dead as a crow," roared Fearchair furiously, "for he is truly a son of the devil. He stole my shot, and spoiled my nights sport. I wish that he and J— K— and M'K— of F—, were burning in the flames of hell. I could willingly sit beside them to see them properly punished." It would appear that J— K— and M'K— of F—, were as bad as "Nossing" for teasing the Wanderer. Fearchair's plan for smoking the rooks was, to place a quantity of sulphur at the bottom of the trees on which they were perched, and to set fire to a long paper match the end of which was to be placed in the sulphur, where, by inhailing the fumes the rooks would become giddy and fall down, and then become an easy prey.

CHAPTER IV.—Self-esteem.

No Beggar—Or Pauper—New Shirts—Fine Sport—English Sermons—Burnt Bannocks—The Inquisitive Pig—Shaving—The Laird's Fool—The Poor's Money—The Tender Passion—Chief of the Clan.

It has already been indicated that Fearchair-a-Ghunna entertained no mean opinion of himself, and numerous stories are told of the naive manner in which he sometimes made this known. He called one day at the kitchen door of a certain farmer's house in the parish of Redcastle, and, the girl in charge having offered him the usual allowance of cake given to members of the wandering class, he indignantly refused it saying, "I will not take it because you're treating me as if I were a beggar." "No, no, said the girl, I don't put you on a level with that class of people. On the contrary, I consider you a real gentleman." "You are a good girl," said Fearchair, as he patted her on the shoulder. "Give me the cake." He got it and ate it heartily.

A farmer from the parish of Petty who was going to Fairburn, met with a woman belonging to the parish of Redcastle, and, as she was going the same road with himself for some distance, they walked together. When near Redcastle they came upon Fearchair, who was sitting at the road side with his load of iron and bones on his back. The woman, after talking with him for a short time, at length suggested he should apply for parochial relief. He at once got into a passion, indignantly repudiating any such idea, and declaring that, he was far above taking anything of the kind. The woman, being acquainted with him, then offered him a few coppers, and the Petty farmer offered him a sixpenny piece, but he would take neither, saying that he was no beggar, but a strong and independent man, who required assistance from no one. "Had you offered me the money to buy powder or shot," he added, "I would have taken it."

A Ferrintosh lady, who had taken some considerable interest in Fearchair's bodily comfort, gave a small sum of money one day to a dressmaker, Mrs Mackenzie, who then resided and still resides at Tore Gate, to purchase cotton and make a couple of shirts for him. On finishing the shirts, Mrs Mackenzie sent a message to Fearchair, that she wished to see him. He went, and being told why he was sent for, he immediately asked how she had got the shirts—whether she got them from the (Parochial) Board. He said:—

"If you got them from the Board you may keep them yourself, as I will have nothing to do with them."

Mrs Mackenzie assured him that the Board knew nothing about them. Wishing apparently to take advantage of the dressmaker, Fearchair then declared that he would only take the shirts on condition that she would wash them for him when dirty. This the woman consented to do, and he took them.

He called at the same lady's house at Tore-Gate on a New-Year's day, and the door happening to be shut at the time, he began to knock at it somewhat lustily, but as the inmates were busy at the time, the door was not opened so readily as Fearchair expected. This greatly disconcerted him, and he knocked at the door with greater force than before, saying :—

"Oh! won't you open the door to me, my dear friends, seeing that I have succeeded in making such a fine shooting."

He had a dead crow, which he had picked up by the way, in his hand, and hence his exclamation regarding his sport.

He frequently attended the English services in the Church of Redcastle, while the late Rev. John Kennedy lived, and, being asked why he did so, seeing that he could not understand a word of English, he answered proudly :—

"I am trying to be like my equals, the rest of the gentlemen in the country. There is no pride in going to hear a Gaelic sermon, to which only common people listen."

He was going on another Sabbath day to hear a sermon on the occasion of a Sacramental Communion at Redcastle, and having been overtaken on the road by a person who was also going thither, the latter addressing him said :—" You are going to church to hear a sermon to-day, Fearchair." " No, I am not " he replied, " but I am going to the box for that purpose." Fearchair, as already mentioned, could understand Gaelic only, and on such occasions as that referred to, Gaelic congregations in the north always worship in the open air, a wooden tent being provided for the clergyman, out of which he addresses the people. Hence Fearchair's allusion to the " box," in his answer.

The Ross-shire Wanderer called one day at a certain farmer's house in the parish of Redcastle, and the servant in charge gave him a basin of broth, but she unwittingly gave him a spoon with a broken handle, and a piece cake which was over-done in the cooking. Fearchair looked at the spoon and bread for a second or so, and then said :—

" A broken spoon and a burnt bannock are things of little value, and things which should never be offered to a gentleman.' Then, entering apparently into the spirit of prophecy, he addressed the girl thus:—" But as you have given such things to me, a broken spoon and burnt bannock will be your partner through life."

With such opinions of his own status it was only what might be expected if he was bitter in resenting an insult, and the incidents recorded of his early life show that he was naturally prone to take revenge. The following incidents show that he was both sensitive and vindictive.

Being on one of his customary tours in the parish of Kirkhill, he got a night's lodgings in a cottar's house at Inchberry. A bed of straw was prepared for him on the floor in a corner of the kitchen. The sole occupant of the cottage was an old woman, who kept a pig, and this animal was quietly sleeping in a wisp of straw close to Fearchair's "shake-down." Towards morning the pig became restive, and at length, finding it had a neighbour, it began to take observations, which were anything but agreeable to Fearchair, especially when it commenced to poke his nose with its snout. "No one is in the habit of kissing me," said he, addressing the pig, "and I will not allow you do it a second time." He immediately rose, seized porky by the hind legs, and knocked out its brains against the wall of the house. "Wife, wife," he exclaimed leaving the house at once, "your black pig is in a fearful fit of rage." He told afterwards that he killed the pig, because the old woman put him to sleep with it. "I'll bet a penny," said he, "she'll not do it again."

He was on another occasion passing a camp of tinkers on the heights of Kilcoy. The tinkers began to make fun of poor Fearchair, and asked him among other things, why he was not shaving. He answered that he was better at shaving others than himself, that it was with his knife (which he took out of his pocket and exhibited) that he usually shaved, and, that he would gladly show his skill on any of them at that moment. The tinkers wisely declined his services as a barber, but in order to make further sport of him, they told him to shave their horse which was grazing close by, and which was more needful than any of themselves. Fearchair agreed, and began operations, but immediately cut the animal's throat. "Accidents happen, to the most skilful," said Fearchair, smiling in a manner altogether peculiar to himself, when he saw the blood gushing out of the wound, but as soon as the animal fell he ran off, shouting "that's capital. When you mock again, try your skill on a greater fool than Fearchair." It is fully believed that he would have treated the tinker who spoke in the same manner as his horse, had he trusted himself into his hands.

There was a time when every family of rank in the Highlands had its fool—generally a feigned one, and, the Highland Laird's Fool was usually considered the wisest man on his estate. He, therefore, always sat next to his lord on the *duis*, and dressed second to none in the family. The fame of Fearchair's wit soon spread far and wide, and as a consequence, rich and poor, young and old, eagerly sought his society, of which no one, until he lapsed into old age, ever tired. A certain laird, residing on the western confines of the Black Isle, took a particular liking to him, and resolved to make him his fool. So the next time Fearchair called at the Big House, he was most sumptuously entertained, after which he gave ample proof of his wit. The laird was so pleased, that he caused Fearchair to be forthwith attired in an excellent suit of clothes, and then told him, that he was to remain with him and share the comforts of the Big House, henceforth while he lived. " I will stay in no man's house longer than I choose," said Fearchair, as he unceremoniously threw off the suit of fine clothes, and donned his old ragged garments. " I will stay with no man, for I am a hunter, as you know, and I will travel through the country with my gun, like all other gentlemen." Fearchair at once left the Big House, and it is said, that he never again visited it. Although the laird was greatly disappointed by Fearchair's contemptuous refusal of his proffered kindness and preferment, he, nevertheless, shewed a hearty interest in him every time he met him on the public road thereafter.

Fearchair's repugnance to become a recipient of Parochial relief is, perhaps, more clearly demonstrated by the following incident than any other. A certain Black Isle gentleman, who is still living, met Fearchair one day and made him a present of a pound note. This circumstance having come to the knowledge of his neighbours some of them determined to tease him, so they said—" you have taken the poor's money at last Fearchair—it was it that Mr G— gave you." This he stoutly denied, declaring it was a pre-

sent; but on their insisting that it was the
poor's money, he directly proceeded to his
donor's residence and proffered him the pound
note saying :—

"Do you think Sir, it would be right of me,
who am able to carry a hundred weight of iron
from Fortrose by Beauly to Inverness, to take
Parochial relief? I will do no such thing."

The gentleman assured Fearchair that he had
given him the pound note as a present, and that
it had nothing to do with Parochial matters.
He was at length persuaded to retain the pound,
and pay no heed to what silly people might say.
Fearchair returned to Tarradale with the note
and a light heart to the bargain. He frequently
afterwards said that Mr G— was the best and
greatest gentleman in the country.

Fearchair-a-Ghunna was at one time under
the sway of the tender passion A certain
young lady, of a prepossessing appearance, lived
in the western district of the Black Isle, for
whom our hero expressed a particular fondness.
This fact coming to the knowledge of some light-
headed youths in his neighbourhood, they re
solved to chaff and tease him about her. They
even questioned his ability to address her
properly. They said—"you will not know when
you call upon her what to say to her, Fearchair."
He answered them snappishly—" I never heard
of any one who went wrong on that score.
Did you?" Being pressed to tell what he
would say, if he went to "pop" the question,

he said, " I would just tell her my position in life—that I am a gentleman—a real hunter—that I am in love with her, and then say—Will you marry me my bonny lass, and be a hunter's wife?"

It is well known that every Highland Sept or Clan had a Chief in Olden times; who occupied that important position in the Clan MacLennan we are not able to say; but Fearchair-a-Ghunna frequently declared, that he himself was the "Chief of the Clan Maclennan," and when he thus considered himself the principal individual of his race, we need not wonder that he should spurn Parochial relief.

CHAPTER V.—INGENUITY.

A Merry-go-round—Fortifying the Garrison—An Emeny's Cornfield—Sanctifying the Sabbath—A Blaster's Device—An Iron Comforter—Hoarding—Pilfering.

Like many ill-balanced minds, Fearchair's was capable of much subtilty, and sometimes showed extraordinary inventive power. A Ferrintosh Farmer took him at one time into his service as herd, a duty which he satisfactorily performed till the Sunday of the Sacramental Communion in the " Burn." He wished much to be with the thousands who worshipped God there that day, but as there was no kind of enclosure for the horses and cattle, he could not possibly leave them. He, therefore, set his wits going, and, he soon hit upon the following plan. He tied horses and cattle head to tail, no easy task, so that they formed a large circle. He then set off to the " Burn," while his charge kept going round and round in the same path till observed by some parties going home from the preaching in the evening, when the poor brutes were released.

Fearchair was frequently annoyed in the

"Garrison" by a lot of neighbouring boys, who delighted in teasing him. One day a man who happened to pass near the "Garrison," was astonished to see Fearchair on his knees near the door, evidently busy, doing something. In order to satisfy his curiosity, the man approached him, and found that he was carefully sticking pins, points upward, in the ground, in a zigzag line. On his asking Fearchair what he meant by so novel a proceeding, he answered:—

"I am every night tormented by a lot of impudent bare-footed boys, and I am placing these pins in the ground, in order that, when the boys come again, they may be punished, for the pins, will without fail, pierce their feet."

But Fearchair had other, and more important motives for sticking the pins in the ground than for punishing the boys. A half-witted fellow, called Donald Coll, who hailed from the neighbourhood of Conon bridge, used to go every Saturday evening to Fearchair's house to make sport of him. Coll was fleet as a hind, so that Fearchair could not catch him, though he often tried to do so. He also was bare-footed, and, it was more especially to punish him that Fearchair put the pins in the ground.

The next Saturday evening after the pins had been put in position, Fearchair, placing himself behind his door patiently waited for Coll's arrival. Immediately he came he was pricked to the quick, and roared in agony. As soon as Coll was pierced, Fearchair, who was armed with a sickle, rushed out to him, with the full intention of cutting off one of his arms, which he positively would have done, but for the timely arrival of a neighbour, who prevented him from carrying his purpose into practice. Fearchair was a good deal annoyed by this neighbour's interference in the matter.

Although there was no great danger of any person entering Fearchair's " Garrison " in his absence, and, although there was neither lock nor bar on its door, it was nevertheless, well provided against any sudden, or unexpected visit. Fearchair had the blade of a scythe fixed in such a manner above the door, that when opened by any person but himself, the blade would come down in guillotine style, and do mortal injury. They were few, however, who darkened his door at any time, and these few did so out of curiosity. No one ever entered the house in his absence, but on one occasion, a neighbour collected some cart loads of bones and other filthy matter which was lying about the house, causing a disagreeable smell, and he poured it into a pit in the neighbouring wood. On discovering this, Fearchair became furious, declaring that he would be revenged on the man for interfering with his goods. As he could not wreak his vengeance in any other way, he went to the man's cornfields, and stuck a number of iron spikes and pieces of wire among the corn. This had the desired effect, for when the man began to shear his corn, his

F

scythes were quite destroyed.

Fearchair frequently went on Sundays to a certain gentleman's residence to get his dinner, but before giving it to him, the servants were in the habit of making him go for coals to the cellar. Having no great liking for work at any time, and the coal cellar being difficult of access, this Sunday employment was anything but congenial to his mind; and he soon contrived a plan for escaping it. He went one Saturday evening to the house in question, and told the servants, that he had come to inform them, that the following day was Sabbath. "Be prepared for it," he continued, "as no work must be done on that day—have all the coals you may require for Sabbath in their proper place on Saturday." "He did not give these instructions," says our informant, "for any special regard he had for the Sabbath, but in order to avoid the carrying of the coals, which he was compelled to do, ere he got his dinner." His device was crowned with success.

Fearchair continued to take an interest in blasting stones till within a short period of his death. A few months prior to that event, he was blasting a stone for a neighbour at Tarradale. The stone being very hard, Fearchair took a longer time to bore it than he anticipated. It was consequently dark, ere he was ready to put in the charge, and the operation was postponed till next day. When he prepared to go home, some of the youths who were looking on said that, they would put the charge in and fire it. " You won't do that," said Fearchair, as he proceeded to fill up the hole with clay, which he pressed so hard, that it took him a considerable time next day to clear it.

We may mention here that Fearchair had an apprehension, that his death would come by the hand of an assassin, and to provide against this, he had several pieces of chain rolled round his neck. These chains, which were constantly worn, were as bright and glittering as silver, and were as much prized by him, as if they had been made of gold.

As he never spent any of the pennies and sixpences he received from the charitable public, nor of the proceeds of his peculiar wares (except the little he paid for powder and shot), he was able to save a considerable sum of money from time to time. But no person had the remotest idea of the place where he kept it, that Fearchair kept a profound secret. When asked by a certain party, where he stored his pelf, he answered wittily :—" I have it buried in a hole in the earth ; and, when I am laid in my grave, my money will lie where it is, concealed and forgotten." As he predicted, the money, so far as known to us, has not been discovered to the present day. He hid a good many other curiosities in the same way.

Fearchair-a-Ghunna was of considerable service to his neighbours at Tarradale, for he would thrash any amount of corn for them, for a merely nominal remuneration. He was at one time thrashing some oats for his next door neighbour, and the landlady noted that after his coming to the barn, she failed to find a single hen's egg. Although she did not suspect Fearchair of having anything to do with the disappearance of the eggs, she, nevertheless, determined to watch his movements on a certain day. Fearchair's work that day was smashing bones in the barn, close to where the hens roosted. The landlady had not been long watching his proceedings, when she saw him go to the hen's nest, and she at once shouted—"what are you doing there Fearchair?" He immediately answered:—" you are very sharp woman. It is only a bone that sprang from the floor to the nest, and I am just taking it out of it." But having had her suspicions thus aroused, the woman was not so easily deceived as Fearchair imagined. She resolved to keep a sharp watch upon him, while he remained at her premises. The result was, that when he was leaving for home, she noticed that he went to a thicket of broom, which grew in rear of the house, and carried something away. She at once ran after him, and found that he was carrying a pot, which was three-fourths full of eggs. This circumstance shows that, Fearchair was not strictly honest in his latter days. It shows furthermore, that he was in no way influenced by that piety which his answers to the clergy, and his ejaculatory prayers indicated. The above is the only instance of his dishonesty that we have heard of, and but that we have received the information from a son of the woman referred to, we would have been reluctant to put it on record.

Fearchair, who was often out for a whole night in search of game in his own peculiar way, came one cold drizzly morning to a certain cottage which stood at the foot of the hill on which he had been engaged in a fruitless hunt all night. The sole occupant of the cottage was a maiden lady, and Fearchair conceived the idea that if he could get into the woman's warm bed (she had not then risen), he would get the warmth and sleep of which he stood in need. For this purpose he forced his way into the cottage, and without any further ado, threw off his wet garments and jumped under the blankets beside the astonished woman, who, with one bound sprang to the middle of the floor, pouring a volley of her choicest Billingsgate on the Wanderer's head for his unseemly conduct. He thanked her kindly for leaving the bed to himself, and then told her that as he was bent on having a snooze she might dry his clothes at the fire.

CHAPTER VI.—QUAINT REMARKS.

Satan's Hair—A Big Fool—Where God is not—Religious Topics—Keen Scent—Disturbing the Congregation—The Miller's Swine—The Belle's Likeness—Education—a Scanty Allowance—The Hearse—Hornless Sheep—Wasps and Good Boys—The Parish Minister—The Cat's Sabbath—The Devil's Funeral.

Fearchair-a-Ghunna had not been long settled in the Black Isle when the fame of his wit and sarcastic answers, had spread far and wide, and often formed the topic of conversation at many a gathering during the long winter nights. Hundreds of people who had never seen him, enthusiastically applauded his sayings, and many bets regarding his merits and demerits, were won and lost at these gatherings. An arrogant young man in the west end of the Black Isle, who ridiculed Fearchair's wit, as well as the sagacity of those who came in contact with him, one night wagered ten to one, that he would give the Wanderer a question, which he could not answer. The bet was taken, and Fearchair was asked to go next evening to a certain house close at hand. Fearchair went, and a large number of people assembled to hear the question and the answer. Immediately on Fearchair being seated, the hero of acuteness asked him, " what is the colour of Satan's hair ?" Without a moment's hesitation Fearchair said :—

" Are you so long in the devil's service, and don't know the colour of your master's hair yet ?" He then looked round the company and burst into a hearty laugh, in which he was joined by all present, his questioner included.

A certain lady meeting Fearchair one day, asked him how it happened that he was such a big fool. He answered readily :—

" Oh ! it is my father's fault. He knew I was fond of the gun and venison, and, in teaching me to shoot rooks, he made a fool of me, but not such a big one as you are." The lady resolved never to ask such a question again.

On another occasion a young man meeting Fearchair addressed him thus :—" Of all the fools I ever saw, I think you are the greatest." The Wanderer replied—" I believe you think yourself a very wise man ; but with all your wisdom and ingenuity, and my apparent silliness try if you can cheat me. If you succeed, I will give you a crown.' The man admitted that Fearchair was right—that he could not be cheated. This man and the subject of our sketch were familiarly acquainted since they were boys.

Being on one of his customary rounds, one day, he was met on the public road by a certain Ross-shire clergyman, who having heard about the Wanderer's wit, asked him if he knew where

God was. Fearchair at once answered—

"Oh! what a fool you are—can you tell me where He is not?"

"You are quite right Fearchair," observed the minister. "God is every where, and we should always remember, that His all-seeing eyes are upon us."

"I don't think God is in every place," said Fearchair, as he moved away.

Among others who heard of the manner in which Fearchair silenced the minister, was the miller of Redcastle, a shrewed, intelligent man. Thinking to puzzle Fearchair the next time he came round, the miller determined to ask him the question which he himself had put to the clergyman. Shortly afterwards Fearchair called at the miller's house, and as soon as circumstances would permit, the latter asked Fearchair if he could tell him of any place where God was not. He answered immediately—

"God is not in the heart of an unconverted man." "Well, well," said the miller, "what a wonder, Fearchair, that the minister did not think of that."

Some strange ineptitude seemed to be connected with the manner in which the clergyman interrogated Fearchair. He called one day at the manse of a well known Ross-shire minister, and after being hospitably entertained, the minister asked him if he was afraid of death. "No, indeed, I am not," was Fearchair's reply. "Does anything at all frighten you?" asked the other in astonishment. Oh! yes. I am afraid of that which is beyond death," answered Fearchair, assuming his interrogator's Sunday gravity.

Having called at the same manse on another occasion, the clergyman, no doubt struck with Fearchair's former laconic answer, was determined to give him a puzzler for once, at anyrate. He, therefore, asked him, if he could tell him, how many miracles Christ performed while He was on earth.

Ubh, ubh, said Fearchair in amazement. *Ciod a rinn E ach miorbhuilean fhad's a bha E air an talamh?* or, "what did He do but miracles while He was on the earth?"

A horse died at one time near a road some little distance south-east of Inverness, and, as was the practice in rural districts in those days, the carcase was allowed to lie where the animal expired, until the dogs devoured all the flesh. Hearing that the bones were bare and clean, Fearchair appeared on the scene, and, gathering the whole of them together, he carried them on his back to Inverness. On his way thither, he was met by a farmer from the estate of Inches who said—"You have a nasty and heavy burden on your back, Fearchair." The latter replied— "I have a more ugly and greater burden than what you see, my good man." "What is that?" asked the farmer. "It is the fearful burden of sin which I constantly carry," said Fearchair, and passed on with his load of bones, and sold them in Inverness, as usual, at a fair price.

While Fearchair had at the manse of Redcastle possession of an out-house which he had filled up with bones, rags, iron, rooks, and frogs, the minister, Mr Macrae, who had been settled there after the Disruption, peeped one day into Fearchair's dwelling, and said :—

Fuigh, fuigh, 'sann agad tha 'm faileadh, Fhearchar."

Fearchair answered :—

Tha iad 'g innseadh dhomhsa gum bheil faileadh maith aig na feidh, ach tha faileadh ni's fearr agadsa, nuair a fhuair thu faileadh stiopain a Chaisteal-Ruaidh 'n America. Which may be translated thus :—

Faugh! Faugh! you have a very bad smell, Farquhar." " They tell me (said Farquhar) that the deer have a keen scent; but you have keener, when you scented the Redcasele stipend from America." The Gentleman in question had come from America to fill up the vacant charge, and hence Fearchair's cutting answer.

Being asked one day shortly after the vacancy caused by the Disruption had been filled up at Killearnan, why he did not attend the Established Church there as formerly, he gave a peculiar look to his interrogator, and replied significantly :—

" I refrain from going to that Church now, because if I did so, the *whole* congregation (which don't, I am told, outnumber the toes of my left foot) could not help looking at me. They would, therefore, lose the benefit of the eloquent and impressive sermon preached by the worthy and esteemed keen-nosed clergyman"

In the above answer, Fearchair sharpened his arrow and shot it with a vengeance

Fearchair having called at a certain miller's house in the Black Isle on one occasion, the miller enquired if he could mention any particular thing he knew. Upon Fearchair replying in the affirmative, the miller asked him what it was. He answered sharply:—

"I know that your swine are in excellent condition."

Reversing the question, the miller asked him—"Can you tell me something that you don't know?" Fearchair answered :—

"Pugh, man, that is an easy matter. I don't know whose corn feeds your swine." This was a retort which the honest miller neither expected nor deserved, for, although it might truly apply to some other millers it did not to the miller in question.

On another occasion Fearchair called at a certain house in the same parish at the dinner hour, and, he happened to be at the time very hungry. One of the landlord's daughters, a haughty, conceited young woman, chanced to be in the kitchen when Fearchair entered it. After making ridicule of him a little while, she offered him a herring. Looking intently at her for a moment, he said :—

"Keep it carefully as a memento of yourself, young woman ; for, every time you look at its scales you will see a perfect likeness of your own beauty, of which you think so much, but of which other people think very little."

An eminent Ross-shire clergyman, famed for his humorous wit and inexhaustible store of anecdotes, was on one occasion taking an evening walk on the public road some short distance from his manse, when he came upon a horse shoe lying on the road. Happening at that moment to see Fearchair coming towards him in the distance, and knowing that he had a peculiar liking to old iron, the minister lifted the shoe and carried it in his hand till he met Fearchair, when he handed it to him saying— "Here is a horse shoe for you Fearchair, which I found on the road a little way back." On receiving the shoe, Fearchair looked intently at it for some moments, and then said :—

"What a grand thing education is! The knowledge it gives a man is really wonderful. I would not know this from a mare's shoe." The clergyman smiled and said, "O Fearchair, Fearchair," and then passed on.

An anecdote somewhat similar to the preceding one appears in "Jamie Fleeman."

There was nothing Fearchair disliked more than to receive a scanty allowance of provision when he called at a house. He called one day at a house in Tarradale in the landlady's absence and, being pretty hungry at the time, he asked a blooming young girl, who chanced to be in the house, to give him something to eat. Flora cheerfully gave him as much cake as she thought was sufficient to satisfy him for the time being, but Fearchair thought otherwise, for, immediately he got it he said :—

"I am afraid my young girl, that you have committed two irreparable wrongs by giving me so much bread. In the first place you have injured yourself by the weight of it; and, in the second place, you have ruined this family by giving so much of their effects away."

Jogging along the public road one day, Fearchair saw a hearse, the first one he had ever seen, approaching him. He asked a man who had just come up to him, what it was. Having been told, he wetted one of his eyes with a spittle, and, as the hearse came up to him, he called out with a lamentable cry, "Oh! dear me, what is this I see? surely it is one of the black coaches of hell." "The tears are only coming from one of your eyes, Fearchair," said one of the men who was along with the hearse. "Och, Och," was Fearchair's ready reply, "the other eye is so stubborn, that it will not shed a single tear."

When walking on one of the public roads in the Black Isle one day, Fearchair met a large drove of sheep. When the rear of the drove had passed him, a farmer appeared on the scene, and addressing the man in charge of the sheep said :—"What a beautiful flock of wedders you have got." They will be of little use to the tinkers," shouted Fearchair, who heard the remark. The point of the observation was that the sheep were hornless.

Being resting at the road-side one day, Fearchair began to sort his bundle as was his wont. He was thus engaged when a wag noticed him and played him a trick. Fearchair was sitting at the side of a bush and the wag tied him to it and then stepped aside to see the result. When Fearchair was sufficiently rested he prepared to go, but was, of course, unable to move from the place where he was sitting. Every time he attempted to rise he failed. He at length muttered to himself, "*Nach mi tha fas lag!*" or, "How weak I am getting!" But finding the trick he vowed vengeance on its author sooner or later.

He was one day, towards the end of summer, passing the parish school of Urray. That summer having been unusually dry, there was a large number of wasp pots throughout the country. At the road side near the school referred to was a pot of great size, and, on seeing Fearchair passing, it occured to some of the biggest school boys to play him a trick. They therefore, induced him, under some pretext, to sit down close to the wasps' pot. As soon as he had done so, the boys struck the pot with their sticks, and hundreds of wasps were instantly flying about Fearchair's face, but strange to say, none of them attempted to sting him. He sat quite composed, looking at the boys, who were standing at a considerable distance off, laughing at, as they supposed, his great dilemma. Wishing, no doubt, to be revenged upon them for the trick, he endeavoured to coax them to come and sit beside him, by offering a penny to each of them, an offer which they wisely declined. Seeing this he said :—" The wasps will not injure you, for you are good boys— they will only hurt the devil's children." Hearing this, and being ashamed of what they had done, the boys immediately skulked away. This anecdote is told by one of the boy's in question—now a gray haired man, and in a good position in life.

Fearchair bore a special hatred to wasps, which was evinced by the determined manner in which he set about destroying them when he chanced to find a "pot" by the wayside. It was no unusual thing to see him spending a long summer's day, in his efforts to kill those little, and (when interfered with) vicious insects—a work in which he took immense delight, and which was carried on thus :—As soon as he found a wasp's "pot," he would set his gun in position—an operation which generally occupied from forty minutes to an hour—the muzzle being placed almost close to the centre of the "pot." This done, the explosion was effected in the customary way, by applying the peat, or match to the priming. But, although the most of the "pot" and the wasps it contained at the time of the explosion, would be burned, or driven to atoms, yet as hundreds of those industrious creatures would at that time be absent on the duties of their domicile, and returning in dozens every minute, a large number would be buzzing at the site of the "pot," ere Fearchair could congratulate himself on its destruction. As it would be useless to attack them with his gun now, and being determined to annihilate them, he would set to, and continue killing them, one after one, with a broom branch, untill the whole were destroyed. It was somewhat remarkable that, although mad with rage for being molested, the wasps were never known to sting him—"*bha sian air*," or he was enchanted.

A certain Ross-shire minister intimated in his church one Sabbath, that he would be preaching in a particular part of his parish on a certain day, but between the time that he intimated this and the day appointed, he received an urgent call to go elsewhere, and consented to go. The minister, of course, made this last arrangement as public as possible. There were some, however, who did not get notice, and Fearchair was among them. He went to the place and remained strolling about the "tent" all day. Shortly afterwards the minister met him, and asked him why he seemed so dull and displeased. "No wonder although I should be sad," said Fearchair, "seeing that the devil makes our parish minister tell lies.

Passing through the Kilcoy district one day, Fearchair called at a house, and as soon as he

entered it, he placed a dead crow, which he had picked up by the way, on the red hot coals. Whenever the flesh began to broil, the flavour spread through the house, and soon reached the nose of the cat, to whom it was apparently very agreeable, for it commenced to mew lustily. Hearing which Fearchair exclaimed angrily:—
 "Hold your tongue, you thief! You need not ask for any of my flesh, for you can kill plenty of rats and mice on Sabbath, which I cannot do."

The Wanderer happened to be standing at the village of Tarradale when the first train that ran on the Ross-shire line passed that village. On seeing it coming along at full speed from the south, he cried :—
 "There comes the devil and his angels—the black messengers of death." That the train has been the "black messenger of death" to hundreds of the human race cannot be denied. He was standing on the bridge that spans the railway at Tarradale on another occasion, and as the train came rushing along from the north, he compared it to "Old Nick's funeral."

"I wonder much," he said one day to the Ferrymen at Kessock, who were teasing him without any mercy, "I wonder much that you will not leave me alone, seeing God Himself is putting up with me so long."

He got a quantity of powder one day from some of the men working in the quarry of Tarradale, who told him to tell no one where he got it. Shortly afterwards he called at the house of a neighbour who knew of his getting the powder from the quarrymen, and to test his powers of secrecy he asked Fearchair where he got the powder. After receiving various evasive answers the neighbour at length said, " Is it not from the men in the quarry you got it Fearchair?" " Well, well, leave it there itself then," said the latter, " and be done with it."

CHAPTER VII—GRAVITY AND DEATH.

Religious Ideas—Sabbath Observance—Time for Church—The Indian Princess—In a Thunderstorm—At Funerals—Prayer—Last Sickness—Blasting again—The Master Passion—The Infirmary—The End.

In spite of all his foibles Fearchair's mind was of a strongly religious cast. His religion moreover was of the sternest kind, for he was firmly convinced that he was by nature an heir of eternal perdition. He belevied that an offended God rules in heaven and earth, who will certainly punish the wicked and unbelieving, but it cannot be said that, his walk and conversation were to any great extent influenced by this belief. His notions of an over-ruling providence may be gathered from the following anecdote. A number of Tomich boys were one day teasing him unmercifully, on which Fearchair-aGhunnan ejaculated the following expressive prayer :—

"O Lord! what canst thou not do to us? Thou art able to thrust us out through the doghole. And then bedaub us in the dung-hill-pit, and all for our sins." The dog-hole, it should be explained, was a hole left in olden times in the masonry at the side of the door, to let the dog pass out and in at pleasure.

Fearchair always showed a peculiar regard for the Sabbath, and latterly he showed this feeling by lying in bed during all that day. On being asked his reason for this conduct, Fearchair replied:—" I will not offend God by treading on his ground on the Sabbath day." The real reason, however, was that on that day, a number of idlers gathered about his door, to tease him as soon as he came out.

Fearchair was in Kilcoy district one Saturday evening, and having called at a certain house there, a bed was provided for him, as usual, in the barn. Wondering that Fearchair did not make his appearance in the kitchen at the proper time on Sunday morning, one of the members of the family proceeded to the barn and asked him why he did not get up. " Don't you know, Fearchair," said the young man, " that this is the Sabbath day, and you ought to rise at the proper time like other folk."

"Why, yes, I do know," said Fearchair, assuming the gravity of a saint, " that this is the Lord's day; and don't you know, my young man, that this is the day which God gave to man and beast for rest? I am only taking the rest that God gave me?"

As several of the Kilkoy people, were proceeding to the church of Redcastle one fine Sabbath day, they overtook Fearchair, who was going to the same church, on the road thither.

As is often the case with country people, they were somewhat late, and one of their number addressing Fearchair said:—" Why are you not running, Fearchair? we are very late to-day?" Fearchair, who was walking at his usual pace, answered with an air worthy of the rev. gentleman whom they were going to hear:—

" If the Holy Spirit overtake us, we shall be in good time."

Fearchair was staying at one time, for about twelve months, at a place called Stronchro, in the parish of Urray; and while there, some young men in his neighbourhood, clubbed together, and concocted the following novel plan in order to induce him to attend the services, every Sabbath, in the church of that parish. They called upon him one evening and told him of the immense riches possessed by the pretty, (they knew he was a great admirer of beauty) though dark skinned ladies of eastern climes; that he needed a wife at any rate, and that it would be as well for him to marry a wealthy lady as a woman without means, that if he should marry an Indian Princess, she not only would clothe him in gorgeous apparel, but she would also deck him with many chains of gold, and supply him with a silver gun; and, that if he would consent to attend divine service every Sunday regularly in the church of Urray for one year from that day, they would send for and present him with one of these rich ladies. Fearchair was so captivated with the prospect of getting so much wealth, that he readily agreed to their terms; and never failed, whatever kind of weather prevailed, to put in an appearance in the church of Urray, during the stipulated time. At the year's end Fearchair demanded his rich wife; and, the youths, equal to the occasion, requested him to meet them on the following evening, at the Tailor's house at Aultgowrie, and that he would meet his millionaire. At the appointed time Fearchair and the youths appeared at the rendezvous. They had one of themselves dressed as a female, whose face was carefully blackened with soot; and, this person they presented to Fearchair as his rich Indian wife. On seeing his supposed future partner through life, Fearchair scanned *her* closely, without uttering a word, for about the space of a minute, and then addressing the youths he said:—

Ubh, ubh, a chairdean, nach i tha oilteal dubh? '*Sann oirre tha coltas an uile,* or "Oh! my friends is she not horribly black? She seems evil itself."

Immediately after he had spoken these words, the *lady* addressing him said, that *she* wished to seal their engagement by a mutual embracing of each other; and suiting *her* words by action *she* approached him for that purpose. Seeing this, Fearchair exclaimed wildly:—

Mar fan thu air falbh uam cuiridh mi a mhosg riut—Air sgath Dhia na tig faisg orm— A chairdean, cumaidh uam i. Which may be rendered thus—If you don't keep off from me I will shot you with the musket—For God's sake do not come near me—My friends keep her from me.

The last part of his utterance was addressed to the youths, who were by this time in fits of laughter. Fearchair, as quick as possible put his musket in position, and directly he did so, he applied the fire to the powder in the usual way. Immediately the explosion took place, Fearchair exclaimed in great glee—" *Hala*, that will, I think, satisfy you (the lady) instead of a husband." The " Indian *lady* " ran away, of course, without experiencing the least harm—*she* was neither hurt nor touched by the shot; and the farce thus ended.

He was blasting stones on one occasion close to where a boy was tending some cattle. The charge was exploded in the usual way, and a large splinter of the stone fell close to where Fearchair was standing. " That piece stone came very near you Fearchair," said the boy. " What would you do if it had struck you ?" " God was between me and the stone," said Fearchair, and then laughed.

One day, during a violent and very alarming thunderstorm, some children asked Fearchair, who was in the house along with them, and seemed easy and composed, whether he was not afraid that the lightning would kill him. Assuming a most solemn appearance he replied gravely —" No, indeed, I am not, for if I am killed by the lightning I shall, perhaps get a corner in heaven."

Fearchair attended all the funerals in the district. Having gone to the funeral of a Dowager-lady, who was noted for her hospitality to the poor of the parish, and who had been particularly kind to the Wanderer, he received several glasses of whisky, and a supply of bread and cheese, along with the others who had gathered for the funeral. When the mournful cortege was about to start for the place of interment, Fearchair noticed many poor people weeping. "I am astonished," he said, "how stiff my eyes are—they refuse to shed a single tear. But although my eyes are dry, the sorrow of my heart for my departed benefactress, is; I am sure, far greater than the sorrow of those who make a show of their grief." And, no doubt, Fearchair spoke the real truth, for the sorrow of many is superficial.

The Ross-shire Wanderer's prayer has already been alluded to. We shall now give as complete a version of it as we could obtain, for it is as curious a prayer as ever was written. Every effort has been used to procure a perfect copy of it, but this was very difficult, as no one person could correctly repeat more than one fourth of it. It is also necessary to say that much of its pathos is lost in the translation.

"O blessed Trinity, thou art in America and Australia, and thou art here just now. Thou art like the fish on the hook—the high-tide will not let thee off. (*Tha thu mar an iasg air an*

dubhan:—cha leig an reothairt dheth thu.) O
Thou art the blessed Trinity. Thou art here
just now, and Thou art in the Highlands, and
in Inverness, and on the high steeples. Thou
art here just now, and east at Tain. Thou art
giving slated houses to the big folk, but Thou
has't only given a black sooty bothy to me,
which won't keep out a rain drop—every drop
falling into Fearchair's brochan (gruel.) Bless
the smith who makes the steel which cuts the
iron for to be driven into the stones. *(Beannaich
an gobhadh a dhealbhas a' chruaidh a ghearras an
tiiarunn air son a sparradh anns na clachan.)*
Bless the earth, O Trinity, and the gutter—the
yellow hen with the chickens; the white cow,
the milk, and the sheep—do, O blessed Trinity.
Bless also the horses, carts, ploughs, and harrows,
the oats, barley, and potatoes; the fire, water,
and all kinds of dishes—yes, bless them, O
blessed Trinity. Bless the trees, grass, and
peats; the broom, whins, heather, brackens, and
juniper. Bless likewise, O Trinity, the guns,
powder, and shot; the rooks, magpies, moor-
fowl, patridges, hares and rabbits—do, O blessed Trinity. Bless also the deer, the roes, the
wild ducks and tame ones; the geese, the gulls,
the dogs, and cats, the mice, rats, and moles—
do, O blessed Trinity. Bless likewise, the fish
in the sea, lake, river, and stream; but bless
more especially, the good big herring that we
get with the potatoes. And bless, O blessed
Trinity, the pipes, tobacco, steel, and flints; the

bones, feathers, rags, keys, and iron. Bless also the wood, hemp, cotton, and tea and sugar—although poor Fearchair's share of them be small. Bless every thing, O blessed Trinity, for Thou Thyself has created all.—Amen."

Fearchair, for many years, would readily repeat this prayer, for a few coppers, but he ultimately got so disgusted by people who were anxious to here it, that when told to say it, he would run away in great anger, exclaiming, *B'e urnuigh mo chreich i ; bu mhaith domh nach dubhairt mi riamh i*, or, It is the prayer of my ruin, it were better for me I had never said it.

Highlanders are credited, rightly or wrongly, with being good singers, and fair poets, but whether Fearchair was skilled in the former we have not heard ; and, the following stanza, which we give in his own vernacular Gaelic, will give an idea of his knowledge of the latter :—

> *A chreubhag mo ruin, seall a mach's thu air leth shuil,*
> *A dh-fheuchainn am faic thu pioghaid mo ghaol,*
> *Na'n rocas mor dubh, a dh'eigheas gun sguir,*
> *'N uair tha ca spuinneadh 'm buntata 's corn'*

TRANSLATION—

> O body my dear, look far beyond here,
> And try can'st thou see, though thy eye single be—
> My lovely magpie, or the rook that soars high,
> And plunders potatoes and barley.

A millwright from the district of Culloden was at work on one occasion in a certain part of Redcastle. One Sabbath morning one of the young women in the house where the millwright was staying requested him to go along with her to the barn where Fearchair was sleeping, to hear his prayer. He agreed and they both went to the barn. After some little coaxing on the part of the young lady, Fearchair repeated his prayer—*Urnuigh-na-Creubhaig*, and the solemn manner in which he did so, strange as the prayer was, had the effect of giving him a very high place in the millwright's estimation. He took him to be a real christian. But no sooner did the young lady begin to tease Fearchair, than the millwright changed his good opinion of him, " for he cursed and swore," said the millwright, in the most awful manner it is possible to conceive. He invoked the Almighty to send fire and brimstone speedly to consume both the girl and myself. " I thought every moment an hour till I got beyond his reach. I never heard anything to equal Fearchair's oaths."

When upwards of eighty years of age, Fearchair-a-Ghunna was as keen a sportsman as he had ever been, though scarcely so fit for his favourite employments of shooting and blasting. In the autumn of 1868 he was one day out fishing in the neighbourhood of Fairburn, where he was met by a brother angler who had a flask of spirits. Fearchair was made welcome to the latter, but he was now becoming old and infirm, and the spirits affected his brain more readily than they would have done at an earlier period. The consequence was that in trying to go home he lost his way. Next morning he was found lying in a wood nearly dead from the effects of the over-dose and the subsequent exposure. A kindly neighbour had him conveyed home in a cart, but as has already been shown there were no comforts for the sick in poor Fearchair's house. His bed consisted of formless heaps of rags, and here with little or no attendance or assistance. Fearchair lay for several days thereafter unable to rise.

The state of affairs coming to the ears of Mr Maclennan of Hilton, that gentleman set about getting Farquhar's house cleaned, and his needs properly attended to. But Fearchair's ruling passion was as strong as ever, and he forbade them under pain of his malediction to touch any of his possessions.

A few days after this sickness had commenced, a neighbour, who went to see him, not imagining that his "sickness was unto death," spoke to Fearchair about a large stone which was in his field and which he wished removed if possible. *Cuiridh sinn as di*, or, "we will destroy it," said the sick man; and, although barely able to move by reason of weakness, he proceeded to the stone and commenced boring it. The man, who went along with him, noticed that when he sat down, he could scarcely get up again. He asked him what was wrong with him. Fearchair answered that something wa wrong with him, but that he could not tell what it was. He managed to blast the stone, went home to his house, and again to bed. As he continued to sink he was removed to a neighbour's house, and about a week afterwards he was carried in a cart to the Northern Infirmary at Inverness. He strongly objected to be removed from his own house, declaring that he would return to it as soon as he would be able to do so. But he never did return. While in the Infirmary he became chargeable to the parish of Contin, Ross-shire.

Fearchair had not been long in the Northern Infirmary when he perceived that his end was fast approaching, and he considered it proper to give some instructions regarding his interment. Addressing his attendant one day he said. " I know that I shall never rise off this bed—I am dying, and when I am dead, I wish my body to be buried in the Church-Yard of Strathconon, along with my fathers and kindred. If my request is not attended to, the curses of my soul and body will rest on you."

Fearchair-a-Ghunna died of paralysis on the 21st day of September 1868, in the 84th year of his age.

His remains were interred in the Tomnahurich Cemetery, where neither stone or slab marks his grave. If Fearchair's attendant in the Infirmary had made known his dying request previous to his interment, it is very probable that his injunction would have been attended to, and he would then have been buried in Strathconon, instead of Tomnahurich, but the attendant failed to make known the Wanderer's request, till some time after his demise.

Photographs of Fearchair a-Ghunna may still be had in Inverness and Dingwall. An oil painting of him, set in a gold-gilt frame may also be seen at Clachuile Inn, in the parish of Urray. It was taken by a peripatetic limner, and conveys a very good idea of the subject of our sketch. The greatest difficulty was experienced in getting him to "sit" while his photograph was being taken, and the painting, seemed at one time to be a hopeless enterprise. Both were, however, ultimately produced, and, as we have said, are good likenesses. One of these forms our frontispiece.

www.ingramcontent.com/pod-product-compliance
Lightning Source LLC
Chambersburg PA
CBHW020235090426
42735CB00010B/1696